classical jazz

Arranged by Brent Edstrom

T0083077

contents

ISBN 978-1-70516-275-0

Visit Hal Leonard Online at
www.halleonard.com

World headquarters, contact:
Hal Leonard
7777 West Bluemound Road
Milwaukee, WI 53213
Email: info@halleonard.com

In Europe, contact:
Hal Leonard Europe Limited
42 Wigmore Street
Marylebone, London, W1U 2RN
Email: info@halleonardeurope.com

In Australia, contact:
Hal Leonard Australia Pty. Ltd.
4 Lentara Court
Cheltenham, Victoria, 3192 Australia
Email: info@halleonard.com.au

APRÈS UN RÊVE
(After a Dream)

By GABRIEL FAURÉ

AVE MARIA

By CHARLES GOUNOD
based on "Prelude in C Major"
by JOHANN SEBASTIAN BACH

DANCE OF THE SUGAR PLUM FAIRY

from the ballet *The Nutcracker*

By PYOTR IL'YICH TCHAIKOVSKY

DIE FORELLE
(The Trout)

Music by FRANZ SCHUBERT

GOLLIWOGG'S CAKE WALK

from *Children's Corner*

By CLAUDE DEBUSSY

HABANERA

from the opera *Carmen*

By GEORGES BIZET

20

HUMORESQUE

By ANTONÍN DVOŘÁK

HUNGARIAN DANCE NO. 5

By JOHANNES BRAHMS

IF LOVE'S A SWEET PASSION

from *The Fairy Queen*

By HENRY PURCELL

IN THE HALL OF THE MOUNTAIN KING

from *Peer Gynt*

By EDVARD GRIEG

MARCH
from the ballet *The Nutcracker*

By PYOTR IL'YICH TCHAIKOVSKY

MEDITATION
from *Thaïs*

By JULES MASSENET

MUSETTA'S WALZ
(Quando men vo)
from the opera *La Boheme*

Music by GIACOMO PUCCINI

MUSIC FOR A WHILE

By HENRY PURCELL

THE OLD CASTLE

from *Pictures at an Exhibition*

By MODEST MUSSORGSKY

PAVANE

By GABRIEL FAURÉ

PRELUDE IN E MINOR
Op. 28, No. 4

By FRÉDÉRIC CHOPIN

PRELUDE IN C MINOR
Op. 28, No. 20

By FRÉDÉRIC CHOPIN

To Coda

RÊVERIE

By CLAUDE DEBUSSY

RONDEAU
from the theatre music for *Abdelazer*

By HENRY PURCELL

SALUT D'AMOUR
(Greeting to Love)

By EDWARD ELGAR

68

SANDMÄNNCHEN
(The Little Sandman)

By JOHANNES BRAHMS

SARABANDE
from *Harpsichord Suite in D Minor*

By GEORGE FRIDERIC HANDEL

Subtle jazz interpretation emerges

SICILIANO

from *Flute Sonata in E-Flat Major*

By JOHANN SEBASTIAN BACH

SLAVONIC DANCE

Op. 27, No. 2

By ANTONÍN DVOŘÁK

STÄNDCHEN
(Serenade)

Music by FRANZ SCHUBERT

THE SWAN
(Le cygne)
from *Carnival of the Animals*

By CAMILLE SAINT-SAËNS

SYMPHONY NO. 9 IN E MINOR

("From the New World")
Second Movement Excerpt

By ANTONÍN DVOŘÁK

TO A WILD ROSE
from *Woodland Sketches*, Op. 51, No. 1

By EDWARD MacDOWELL

TRÄUMEREI
(Dreaming)
from *Scenes from Childhood*

By ROBERT SCHUMANN

The Best-Selling Jazz Book of All Time Is Now Legal!

The Real Books are the most popular jazz books of all time. Since the 1970s, musicians have trusted these volumes to get them through every gig, night after night. The problem is that the books were illegally produced and distributed, without any regard to copyright law, or royalties paid to the composers who created these musical masterpieces.

Hal Leonard is very proud to present the first legitimate and legal editions of these books ever produced. You won't even notice the difference, other than all the notorious errors being fixed: the covers and typeface look the same, the song lists are nearly identical, and the price for our edition is even cheaper than the originals!

Every conscientious musician will appreciate that these books are now produced accurately and ethically, benefitting the songwriters that we owe for some of the greatest tunes of all time!

VOLUME 1
00240221	C Edition	$45.00
00240224	B♭ Edition	$45.00
00240225	E♭ Edition	$45.00
00240226	Bass Clef Edition	$45.00
00286389	F Edition	$39.99
00240292	C Edition 6 x 9	$39.99
00240339	B♭ Edition 6 x 9	$39.99
00147792	Bass Clef Edition 6 x 9	$39.99
00200984	Online Backing Tracks: Selections	$45.00
00110604	Book/USB Flash Drive Backing Tracks Pack	$85.00
00110599	USB Flash Drive Only	$50.00

VOLUME 2
00240222	C Edition	$45.00
00240227	B♭ Edition	$45.00
00240228	E♭ Edition	$45.00
00240229	Bass Clef Edition	$45.00
00240293	C Edition 6 x 9	$39.99
00125900	B♭ Edition 6 x 9	$39.99
00125900	The Real Book – Mini Edition	$39.99
00204126	Backing Tracks on USB Flash Drive	$50.00
00204131	C Edition – USB Flash Drive Pack	$85.00

VOLUME 3
00240233	C Edition	$45.00
00240284	B♭ Edition	$45.00
00240285	E♭ Edition	$45.00
00240286	Bass Clef Edition	$45.00
00240338	C Edition 6 x 9	$39.99

VOLUME 4
00240296	C Edition	$45.00
00103348	B♭ Edition	$45.00
00103349	E♭ Edition	$45.00
00103350	Bass Clef Edition	$45.00

VOLUME 5
00240349	C Edition	$45.00
00175278	B♭ Edition	$45.00
00175279	E♭ Edition	$45.00

VOLUME 6
00240534	C Edition	$45.00
00223637	E♭ Edition	$45.00

Also available:
00154230	The Real Bebop Book	$34.99
00240264	The Real Blues Book	$39.99
00310910	The Real Bluegrass Book	$39.99
00240223	The Real Broadway Book	$39.99
00240440	The Trane Book	$25.00
00125426	The Real Country Book	$45.00
00269721	The Real Miles Davis Book C Edition	$29.99
00269723	The Real Miles Davis Book B♭ Edition	$29.99
00240355	The Real Dixieland Book C Edition	$39.99
00294853	The Real Dixieland Book E♭ Edition	$39.99
00122335	The Real Dixieland Book B♭ Edition	$39.99
00240235	The Duke Ellington Real Book	$25.00
00240268	The Real Jazz Solos Book	$39.99
00240348	The Real Latin Book C Edition	$39.99
00127107	The Real Latin Book B♭ Edition	$39.99
00120809	The Pat Metheny Real Book C Edition	$34.99
00252119	The Pat Metheny Real Book B♭ Edition	$29.99
00240358	The Charlie Parker Real Book C Edition	$25.00
00275997	The Charlie Parker Real Book E♭ Edition	$25.00
00118324	The Real Pop Book – Vol. 1	$39.99
00240331	The Bud Powell Real Book	$25.00
00240437	The Real R&B Book C Edition	$45.00
00276590	The Real R&B Book B♭ Edition	$45.00
00240313	The Real Rock Book	$39.99
00240323	The Real Rock Book – Vol. 2	$39.99
00240359	The Real Tab Book	$39.99
00240317	The Real Worship Book	$35.00

THE REAL CHRISTMAS BOOK
00240306	C Edition	$35.00
00240345	B♭ Edition	$35.00
00240346	E♭ Edition	$35.00
00240347	Bass Clef Edition	$35.00
00240431	A-G CD Backing Tracks	$24.99
00240432	H-M CD Backing Tracks	$24.99
00240433	N-Y CD Backing Tracks	$24.99

THE REAL VOCAL BOOK
00240230	Volume 1 High Voice	$40.00
00240307	Volume 1 Low Voice	$40.00
00240231	Volume 2 High Voice	$39.99
00240308	Volume 2 Low Voice	$39.99
00240391	Volume 3 High Voice	$39.99
00240392	Volume 3 Low Voice	$39.99
00118318	Volume 4 High Voice	$39.99
00118319	Volume 4 Low Voice	$39.99

Complete song lists online at www.halleonard.com